DAY TRADING OPTIONS

The Complete day trading crash course for beginners. Learn here all the strategies on how to do it for a living.

Brad Johnson

© **Copyright 2020 - All rights reserved.**

The content contained within this book may not be reproduced, duplicated or transmitted without direct written permission from the author or the publisher.

Under no circumstances will any blame or legal responsibility be held against the publisher, or author, for any damages, reparation, or monetary loss due to the information contained within this book. Either directly or indirectly.

Legal Notice: This book is copyright protected. This book is only for personal use. You cannot amend, distribute, sell, use, quote or paraphrase any part, or the content within this book, without the consent of the author or publisher.

Disclaimer Notice: Please note the information contained within this document is for educational and entertainment purposes only. All effort has been executed to present accurate, up to date, and reliable, complete information. No warranties of any kind are declared or implied. Readers acknowledge that the author is not engaging in the rendering of legal, financial, medical or professional advice. The content within this book has been derived from various sources. Please consult a licensed professional before attempting any techniques outlined in this book.

By reading this document, the reader agrees that under no circumstances is the author responsible for any losses, direct or indirect, which are incurred as a result of the use of information contained within this document, including, but not limited to, — errors, omissions, or inaccuracies.

TABLE OF CONTENTS

INTRODUCTION 6
    CHARACTERIZING DAY TRADING AND DAY TRADING OPTIONS 8
    GETTING MARGIN 11
    HISTORY OF OPTIONS TRADING 12

CHAPTER 1: MINDSET OF A SUCCESSFUL TRADER 14
    CHARACTERISTICS OF A DAY TRADER 14
    DIFFERENCE BETWEEN LONG AND SHORT TRADE 18
    CAN ONE DO DAY TRADING FOR A LIVING? 18
    BENEFITS: 19
    DRAWBACKS: 20

CHAPTER 2: WHAT ARE OPTIONS? 22
    OPTIONS PRICING AND EXPIRATION DATES 24
    BUYING AND SELLING OPTIONS 24
    ADVANTAGES OF OPTIONS 26

CHAPTER 3: THE STEPS NEEDED TO START DAY TRADING OPTIONS 28
    BUILDING UP YOUR WATCH LIST 28
    DECIDE WHICH OF THESE STOCKS WORK BEST FOR YOU 29
    PUT THAT ENTRY AND EXIT STRATEGY IN PLACE 29
    PURCHASE THE STOCKS YOU WANT 30
    PAY ATTENTION 31
    SELL YOUR STOCKS WHEN THEY REACH YOUR ORIGINAL EXIT POINTS 32
    STARTUP YOUR SECOND (AND THIRD AND FOURTH AND SO ON) TRADE 34

CHAPTER 4: THING TO CONSIDER BEFORE YOUR FIRST TRADE 36
    HOW TO CONTROL YOUR EMOTIONS 36
    FEAR 36
    GREED 42
    HOPE 43
    REGRET 44

CHAPTER 5: OPTIONS DAY TRADING STYLES 46
    THE RESISTANCE TRADING STRATEGY WITH OPTIONS 47
    MOMENTUM OPTIONS DAY TRADING 49
    WHAT IS REVERSAL TRADING AND HOW THIS WORKS 50
    SCALPING OPTIONS DAY TRADING 51
    USING PIVOT POINTS FOR OPTIONS DAY TRADING 52

CHAPTER 6: DOES A FUNDAMENTAL ANALYSIS WORK WITH OPTIONS? 56

- CREATING YOUR WATCHLIST FOR POSSIBLE POSITIONS 57
- VALIDATING THE QUALITY OF YOUR POSSIBLE POSITIONS 58
- CHOOSING WHICH POSITION WILL EARN MAXIMUM GAINS (AND MINIMIZE LOSSES) 59
- PICKING YOUR EXACT ENTRY POINT 61

CHAPTER 7: TIPS FOR DAY TRADING OPTION 62

- ALWAYS BE FLEXIBLE WHEN TRADING OPTIONS 62
- WORKING WITH BREAK-EVEN POINTS 63
- ALWAYS DO YOUR RESEARCH 64
- GOING WITH THE FLOW 66
- YOUR EXIT POINT, OR YOUR ESCAPE PLAN 66

CHAPTER 8: THE PSYCHOLOGY OF AN OPTION TRADING 68

- DO NOT RATIONALIZE YOUR TRADING ERRORS 69
- BEWARE OF YOUR TRADING DECISIONS 70
- KEEP YOUR EMOTIONS IN CHECK 72
- BE PATIENT WHEN TRADING 74

CHAPTER 9: RISK MANAGEMENT 76

- MONEY & RISK MANAGEMENT TECHNIQUES 76
- UNDERSTANDING MARGIN TRADING 77
- MANAGE MARKET RISK 79
- RISK MANAGEMENT TECHNIQUES 80
- USING RISK-REWARD RATIO 82

CHAPTER 10: TRADING TOOLS AND PLATFORMS 84

- A PLATFORM TAKES TRADING TO THE HOLDERS 85
- RIVALRY 86
- WATCHLIST AND SCANNERS 87

CHAPTER 11: BUILD YOU TRADING STRATEGIES 88

- BUILDING YOUR OWN ROUTINE 88
- THE 30% RULE 89

CONCLUSION 94

BRAD JOHNSON

Introduction

Day exchanging alludes to the shared buy and offer of monetary instruments during a similar exchanging day, for example, protections, prospects, choices, and monetary standards. Open offers are kept for the time being, once in a while, on the special seasons, or when the market is shut for a vacation. At first, day exchanging was just open to budgetary organizations, principally banks, and business organizations. In any case, with the expanding development of electronic exchanging, which permitted outcasts access to trades and market information, day exchanging turned out to be extremely basic among consultants too, additionally called informal investors starting now and into the foreseeable future. Like in each other type of exchange, day exchange brings a significant hazard, and the results can run from predictable and compensating productivity to monstrous misfortunes.

This is genuine with regards to exchanging intensely utilized budgetary instruments, where the net impact will swing by a large number of dollars inside seconds dependent on the size of the position. Day exchanging is a sort of exchange, which comprises of various sub-exchanging types. They incorporate momentary exchanging, i.e., scalping, including high volume passage and flight of offers, to swing exchanging, where a spot could be left open the entire day to profit by incredible market milk. Sometime, dealers use a mix of exchanging types to accomplish the best outcomes, yet this takes a great deal of training, and extreme fixation two characteristics experienced brokers only here and there have. This is the reason most informal investors incline toward one sort of exchanging, and they focus on different exchanging types.

A few brokers enter just with-design exchanges, and they follow the pattern best for amateur dealers. Conversely, others do extend exchanging enter positions in the two bearings as request swings in a channel with high help rates and opposition. There are additionally amazingly proficient dealers and some very fledgling ones wagering against the market, situating counter-pattern exchanges. Yet, while the expert market members will exploit these high-chance contestants, the novices are simply acquiring substantial misfortunes that will definitely wash their exchanging accounts clean. The accomplished dealers do the supposed opposite wager, accepting that the cost will essentially switch dependent on long periods of experience and complex strategies of research.

Around a similar time, novice brokers are stuck in losing counter-pattern exchanges since they don't understand whether a pattern is high and is bound to endure, as opposed to switching. Numerous informal investors base their choices on news coming out of the day by day exchanging day, including monetary reports that can be remembered for the financial schedule, just as consequences of strategy gatherings and discourses by national banks, priests, and so on. These occasions create huge vulnerability, especially from the significant economies, and offer informal investors a solid possibility of fulfilling profit, and especially hawkers. Informal investors commonly exchange the news understanding with a scope of measurements to improve their outcomes, for example, the Relative Strength Index, Average Directional Movement Index, and so on. Be that as it may, a few other informal investors battle that the improvement of issues is probably going to convey better returns.

They direct the purported exchanging of market movement. That is a strategy centered around specialized research, in which merchants decide if they will enter an exchange concentrated on a blend of value activity. They read bar by bar graphs, patterns, for example, banners, triangles, wedges, head and shoulders, volume, and other crude market measurements. Dissimilar to the day-exchanging types referenced above, showcase activity merchants don't utilize the in any case generally used markers. Value activity brokers will in general overlook all the essential reasons that may impact value development yet depend intensely on the capacity to comprehend human brain research and group conduct that is reflected in the situating of the overall population. This makes value activity.

Characterizing Day Trading and Day Trading Options

The shortsighted importance of fundamental money related subordinate is another option. A common course of action gives you the option to purchase or sell a thing on or during a predetermined date of the activity. In the event that you are the merchant, you are obliged to concur with the details of the agreement. It will be either selling or buying if the client needs to practice the privilege before the expiry date. Day exchanging choices spread various markets. You will get value alternatives, choices for the ETF, choices for prospects, and that's only the tip of the iceberg. Additionally named vanilla choices are such traditional other options. The shortsighted importance of a basic budgetary subsidiary is another option. A common game plan gives you the option to purchase or sell a thing on or during a predetermined date of the activity.

You will locate the Underlying Asset that most choices are based, for instance, on shares in openly recorded organizations, Twitter and Amazon. There is, be that as it may, an expanding number of choices dependent on fundamental elective ventures. These incorporate choices for day exchanging on stock records, monetary forms, items, and venture confides inland (REITs) Stock Options When you are keen on day exchanging investment opportunities professionally, it is significant that the exchanges are centered around the fundamental stock's 100 offers. The exemption to this law is the place the progressions emerging from stock parting and mergers happen. Provincial Variations Most investment opportunities traded available are American ones.

They can be drilled from the date of obtaining before expiry anytime. Be that as it may, European choices must be practiced after the expiry date. Alternatives versus Futures There are numerous contrasts between day exchanging choices and fates that numerous individuals rapidly know. They are typically both dependent on a similar instrument that underlies them. There are likewise a few equals to the structure of the genuine agreements. The qualification is the means by which the exchange happens. You get a more extensive scope of alternatives with the bundles. You'll additionally take note of that the laws of trade are unique. Alternatives can be sold independently, or you can get them with stock exchanges or prospects agreements to make a type of exchange protection.

There are different reasons you may make genuine exchanging open doors for capital. For some alluring components, including putting money related compensation as an afterthought, day exchanging of alternatives advances. More noteworthy Advantages You can profit considerably more from a choice as the stock moves. Suppose a stock moves somewhere in the range of $25 and $50. This will gain you a capital cost of 100 percent. Be that as it may, a call choice going from $1 per agreement to a $5 agreement will offer you an advantage of 500 percent. What's more, with another option, you will procure more and with less time. Alternatives can be effective when different markets battle. Albeit different business sections battle, choices can be effective. Incompletely because that you don't need to utilize the option to make its best.

In addition, vulnerability can be sure for itself. Commonly useful – while investment opportunities are frequently based on, include both and can offer you more advantages. That is on the grounds that you can sell the salary creating directly on stocks you effectively own. The exchanging of intraday alternatives is multifaceted and conveys enormous open doors for advantage with it. Maybe the best perspective convenience.

You can proceed with day-exchanging from anyplace on the planet with alternatives. What you need is to interface with the web. Day exchanging and long haul contributing are likewise possible methods of stock exchanging and numerous dealers are liking to do as such. Day exchanging implies making exchanges that keep going for a considerable length of time or minutes, benefitting from momentary swings in the cost of an advantage. The two records are opened and shut for day exchanging around the same time.

Getting Margin

Day exchanging generally utilizes influence edge during the day of exchange. The edge rates and conditions vary as indicated by the money related instrument of the Stock Margin and the agent. Day exchanging purchasing power for stocks and choices has a loaning proportion of 4 to 1 or multiple times the record's venture edge abundance. In an oversimplified manner, that implies that with the additional money in the portfolio, you can purchase stocks and alternatives at only 25 percent of the market. Benefit surplus is the standard to have customer value beneath obligation. The overnight edge is somewhere in the range of 2 and 1 or 50 percent of the estimation of the position.

Informal investors can fall into traps in the event that they don't have the foggiest idea about the benefit is exclusively at the specialist's tact. Representatives will lessen the portfolio influence proportion to 2 to 1, permitting 50 percent rather than 25 percent surplus value for profoundly unstable stocks. This is a major thought while starting an intraday edge call. The agent is qualified for loosen up a stake, much of the time at the most reduced occasions, when an edge call must be reached. Stockbrokers can urge brokers to control their money and amplify their buying influence intraday.

History of Options Trading

The word day exchanging toward the start of the new thousand years evokes dull recollections of the web bubble bear advertise. Day exchanging was a famous phonon between "1997-2001". At the point when the Nasdaq Composite file took off from underneath 1,000 to more than 5,000 filled by the flood from gadgets and web stocks. Informal investors' features making $5-$10,000 a day ruled the standard and motivated a ton of institutional purchasers to participate in day exchanging. Beginning open contributions (IPOs) available stamping for the time being moguls by barrel standard took off triple digits. Everything stopped as the 2000-2002 bear advertise struck.

The technological bubble sparked a major sell-off in the market when the S&P 500 index collapsed 58 percent. Even worse, the Nasdaq Composite Technology Heavy Index crashed a whopping 78 percent, from a high of 5,048 in March 2000, to a low of 1,114 on October 9, 2002! The various margins call liquidations and horror tales of missing life savings prompted regulatory action, such as PDT Rule 4210. Trading options can be dated back to 332BC, when a man known as Thales bought the right to buy olive before harvesting, reaping a fortune. Options then reappeared during the 1636 tulip mania where tulip options were commonly bought to gamble on the rising tulip quality. Then in London, at the end of the seventeenth century, a market was developed to deal with both calls and put options.

This was the first case of both call selling and putting calls on an exchange. By 1872, Russel Sage launched the unstandardized and illiquid US over the Counter call and put options market. The introduction of options trading as we know it today came with the formation in 1973 the Chicago Board Options Exchange (CBOE) and Options Clearing Corporation (OCC), where structured listed exchange call options were launched. By 1977, the CBOE has launched put options and since then, the stock market has taken on the structured traded form of exchange that we are familiar with today.

Chapter 1: Mindset Of A Successful Trader

Day trading is basically the purchasing and selling of securities within a single trading day in any marketplace at commonly stock markets and foreign exchange (FOREX) for the purpose of obtaining a compound of short term loans. Day traders involved in this are fully investing in this trading activity with multiple learning sources, learning time and good kind of capital often end up being so successful. Being successful in day trading literally means acquiring large chunks of profits amounts.

Characteristics of a Day Trader

Being a day trader does come out naturally, a specific personality and traits are duly required. Below are some of the characteristics of a day trader.

Disciplined.

This is a major trait that day traders really need to input. Day traders should always be disciplined to remain input when no opportunities emerge and really act so fast when opportunities avail. Acting fast also includes strictly considering the step by step rules and obligations initially formed in their big plans.

Open-minded.

Day trading is a learning kind of income-generating engagement, implying that there are going to be happy times and the downfalls. Save yourself and learn from all that. Improve the happy times and completely discard the downfall of wrong moves. Being exposed to the winnings and the failures makes you open-minded, master of all possible win moves.

A Fan Of Technology.

Day trading is carried out in various trading platforms and systems that a trader should be familiarized with. This should not scare you. Getting to know how they work does not, in any case, require you to be a computer whiz. Get to learn the basic moves and grow technologically with time.

Mentally Tough.

Losing market trades are constant; most successful traders will have losing trades every single day. They typically win slightly more times than they lose. It is so important too stay focused and rational during a losing period and do not let in the basic fact that money has been lost too. Focus on the future day trading activities by implementing some of the strategies outlined in a big plan.

Independence.

Independence is striving to build your own toolbox that is and willy forever lead you. Reading trading books to trading books, watching each video, interacting with one mentor after the other can be a total miss. What if different books have one confusing point on a particular field? What is your YouTube subscriber who decides to quit vlogging? Always grasp the basics after in-depth research and day stay put. Dare to yourself that you got you and get the large chunks of benefits. However, when you feel you are so lost, do not hesitate to get assistance. Most importantly, master and analyze successful moves and let them be part of your big plan.

Patience.

Good things do take quite some time. In every strategical move, you try to make, think about it carefully but this should not make you paranoid. Act accordingly with many disciplines to reduce the number of losses likely to be incurred during various day trading activities.

Also, a patient day trader is a learning day trader. Day trading is not going to be easy at first but with time, where you will be equipped with lots of skills and experience, things are expected to flow very smoothly. Hey, be patient.

Future-Oriented.

Getting stuck in the past makes you much of a prisoner. Forward-thinking lets you see the possible moves and gives you the decisive air when the next trading activity will occur considering the set protocols set in the day trader's plan. Being future-oriented incites forward thinking which clearly involves mental thinking and knowing your next possible moves after a considerate examination. Being future-oriented hastens and simplifies the day trading operation moves and chances are that they are going to be successful.

Financial Freedom.

Day trading does not require you to be a tycoon necessarily but you are required to have a specific amount of money that has been precisely selected to begin day trading with. Remember the first times are always a win or loss situation, as you continue to learn and grow. This particular set of money can be lost too. Be careful about how you handle your finances in day trading. Not every story is a good story.

Enthusiasm.

A great interest in something is a pending successful goal. A great enthusiastic inclination to stocks, securities, commodities, markets, the business gives you the thirst to learn and master what day trading is all about. These are signs of a future successful day trader.

Experience and Familiarity.

Experience comes with pretty much of downfall lessons and learning. Expose yourself to different learning sources and master every profitable move during day trading so as to squeeze out the best out of that. Getting the actual experience and familiarity of the trading platforms and various strategies needed to be successful at day trading is worthwhile.

Difference Between Long and Short Trade

In stock markets, the terms long and short basically imply whether a trade was initiated by first selling or first purchasing. A long trade is initiated when the day trader purchases at a particular price with the intention of selling at a higher price in future in a bid to get profits whereas short trades are initiated with selling, before even purchasing with the intention of repurchasing at a lower price from the market and eventually acquire profits.

Short selling is simply:

Borrow the stock.

Sell the stock.

Buyback the stock?

Profit or loss?

Risks are also involved during short selling; stock prices may end up being so high and normally, there is no limit to how a particular price can actually go.

During long trading, your profit potential is unlimited since the price of the asset can rise indefinitely.

Can One Do Day Trading for a Living?

The first point to take down is yes, day trading is a lucrative engagement. However, that does not mean that it is way simple than any other actual job. And yes, you get to be your own boss. You get to do it your way, on your time, with your strategies for a living. It is amazing. We do not get so lucky in this life though, drawbacks have to appear too. Below, let us venture on the different pros and cons that come with day trading.

Benefits:

Own Boss

Getting to work the way you desire has always been the best thing ever. Your plan, your moves, your strategies. This is so good. Imagine going for a wanting vacation without first passing through the Human Resource department with some great explanation so that your reason can be valid enough. Moreover, getting to work for you already gives you the full energy to make things really alive. You have enough spirit to learn and bring out the best in you. Do yourself a huge favor and be your own boss.

Comfort.

A peaceful working environment enhances the quality of the end product, or rather, the aftermath turns out to be so successful. A peaceful environment creates a much-concentrated workspace, day traders get to strictly master the actual day trading activities and learn more every day. This will at the end accomplish their big plans as indicated by the large chunks of profits that would be made.

Risk Management.

Exposure to day to day cases of day trading will definitely make you a better risk-taker. Day trading is made up of so many risks that act as a day to day lessons. The trader gets to master the good moves and discard the previously made mistakes so as to become a successful day trader.

Technologically Advantaged.

Day trading exposes you to the internet as you try to get access to various sources. The internet is technology, so full of technology. You are exposed to new sites and different technological techniques. This builds you because technology is the present and the future.

Drawbacks:

A Solitary Lifestyle.

Day trading is a peace of mind activity implying that physical noise should not be part of it. This creates a lonely kind of environment since the trader is mostly by his or her self trying to master the possible good moves. You are really going to enjoy day trading if the best company is normally just your company.

Inconsistent Salary Figure.

Your smart trading work will be reflected by the salary figure you obtain every single trading day. When you decide to take a day off, no gains are promised. At one particular point, you may gain like $3000 and the next day you experience $2000 loss, no consistent salary figures are promised, your smart moves are the ones that will get you a Lamborghini.

BRAD JOHNSON

Chapter 2: What Are Options?

An option is a contract that gives you the right to buy or sell shares of stock at a fixed price. A single options contract is for 100 shares of stock. So, one option contract might give you the ability to sell a hundred shares of a stock at $100 a share, or it might give you the ability to buy 100 shares of stock at $100 a share. The price that is specified in the contract is fixed, and so it doesn't necessarily matter if the market price of the stock is fluctuating as far as that goes. That is, even if the stock price were to rise to say $200 a share, or even $300 a share, if you have an option that specifies that you have the right to buy 100 shares at $100 a share, that contract must be honored if you choose to exercise it.

Of course, you don't have to exercise it, and that is why they are called "options". It is optional for the buyer to actually exercise their rights under the contract and buy or sell the shares. In fact, many options traders never do so. As the market price of the stock goes up and down, the value of the option itself goes up and down and so there are opportunities to profit merely by trading the options contract itself. This happens on the options exchange. To tell the truth, there are several options markets where options are traded, but as a trader working through a broker that is all hidden from you, and you simply buy or sell your options through the broker without worrying about where they are really traded and who buys or sells the options.

Options can earn profits for people buying or selling them. For this reason, many people enter into an options trade by "writing" or selling to open an options contract. These people, who sell an options contract to open their position in the market, have the highest risk. That is because if you sell to open an options contract you are legally obligated to follow through on that contract. So, if you have sold to open an option to sell 100 shares at a given price, if a buyer decides to exercise the contract, you have to sell them the shares. Likewise, there are certain types of options contracts that require you to purchase shares of stock at a fixed price. If it is profitable for the buyer to do so, they can exercise their rights and decide to sell you the shares, and you must buy them in that case.

That sounds pretty scary, and if you are careless it could get you into trouble. However, as we will see using sound strategies you can sell options at relatively low risk to yourself and earn an income doing so.

As a buyer, you have a much lower risk. Your maximum risk is fixed. This is given by the price you pay for the option. In most cases, this is going to run from $30 or $50 up to a few hundred dollars, although options on highly-priced stocks like Amazon might be pricier. A buyer is normally hoping to earn profits from the price movements of the stock. Since options are traded on their own markets, this means that the prices of options are fluctuating up and down as the price of the stock increase or drops down, and so you can purchase at a low price and sell high with the options without ever actually buying the stock that backs the option.

Options Pricing and Expiration Dates

So, an option is a contract on the shares of a particular stock. That means you might buy an option on Apple, IBM, Boeing, or Facebook for example. However, there is something important you need to know about options. Options come with an expiration date. If an option expires, and you haven't exercised or sold the option, it becomes worthless.

This means that you need to keep a close eye on the expiration dates of any options that you invest in. In addition, you will need a specific plan that will help you decide when to get out of the options contract to either make a profit or to cut your losses.

Sellers need to be aware of expiration dates as well. If an option expires and it is "in the money", which means that it would be advantageous for a buyer to exercise their rights under the contract, then you will have to meet your obligations. That means either buying or selling 100 shares of stock. Most people that sell options get out of their obligation as the expiration date approaches so that they are not put into this position.

Either way, it is important for an options trader to be very aware of the expiration date of any option that they invest in.

Buying and Selling Options

As we mentioned earlier, you can buy to open an options contract, or you can sell to open an options contract. If an options contract is "in the money" this means that the option can be exercised by a buyer to earn a profit, which means either buying or selling 100 shares of stock. On the other hand, if it is "out of the money", then it would not be profitable for the buyer to exercise the option. Sellers of options contracts generally hope that the option will be out of the money. If a contract were to expire and it was out of the money, it is said to "expire worthless". Since the contract has expired without any value, the seller of the option pockets any money they received selling it, and they don't have to worry about buying or selling shares of stock.

A buyer of an option is normally a trader. That means they are hoping to sell it at a higher price than they paid for it. As the price of the stock goes up and down, it can cause the market price of any options contract on that stock to move up or down. This provides traders an opportunity to earn profits without actually investing in the stock. When the value of an option goes up, they can sell the option to another trader for a profit.

Keep in mind that if you buy an option to enter your investment position, you are not under any sort of obligation. In other words, if you later sell the option, you are not under the seller's obligation. Only the original seller of an option is required to either buy or sell shares of stock. So, you can buy an option, and if its value goes up you can sell it off and take a profit and walk away from it. Many people trade options without having any intention to own the shares of stock or trade shares of stock whatsoever. But if you want to, you can definitely buy or sell the shares if it becomes advantageous and you can afford it.

Advantages of Options

Options carry many advantages over trading stock. The first advantage is the amount of capital required to enter into a trade. If you want to buy 100 shares of a stock, and on the market it's priced at $200 a share, that means you must come up with $20,000. But with an option, you can control the underlying shares of stock only investing the small sum of money required to buy an option. For a stock trading at $200, depending on circumstances the price of an option could vary from $150 - $300. That is a lot less than having to come up with $20,000, and as we'll see you can earn huge profits from the price movements of the stock that the option represents without having to come up with huge amounts of capital. For that reason, options trading opens up large profit possibilities for small investors that they would not have otherwise.

Options also allow you to enter into complex trades that aren't possible when investing directly in stock. The advantages of this is that you can setup trades that allow you to earn profits with different types of stock movements. So, you can earn profits if the stock is moving up, if it is dropping, or if it is ranging which means it is staying within a narrow range of prices. You can also make profits if the share price of a stock shoots off in one direction or another

To summarize, options trading lets you get in the market with a small amount of upfront capital, it lets you leverage 100 shares of stock without actually owning it, and you can utilize trading strategies that stock traders are not able to use.

Chapter 3: The Steps Needed To Start Day Trading Options

Building up Your Watch List

The first step when you are ready to get started in day trading is to do some research. When you first wake up in the morning, look over your notes and your research and then use that information to create a good watch list. This watch list can be important because it can limit you down to just a few options that you plan to use for trading on that day. There are thousands of stocks on the market and making this watch list will make it so much easier for you to pick the right stocks to invest in.

Furthermor, there are different methods you can use to create this watch list. But one of the best options is to use a scanner. These scanners can look for specific criteria that you want out of a stock and can make things faster than trying to look through them all on your own. To make the scanner work, you just need to list out the requirements that you want the stock to meet and then the scanner will alert you as soon as it finds one that meets these.

Decide Which of These Stocks Work Best for You

After the scanner has given you a few options for stocks that meet your requirements, you can decide which of these the best stocks are. You may have a specific strategy that you would like to go with and then choose the stock that seems to be following that strategy the best. You can always change strategies from one day to the next, or you can choose to stick with one strategy if it is serving your purpose.

Make sure that you do not trade in the market for at least the first five minutes after the market opens. Some professionals wait even longer than these five minutes for the market to settle down. There can be a ton of commotion and crazy ups and downs in the market during those first few minutes and investing at this time can hurt your profits. If you spend time looking at your scanner and then investigating the stocks that you receive, it will probably be at least five or more minutes before you are ready to enter the market anyway, but it is still important to be aware of this volatility and learn how to avoid it.

Put That Entry and Exit Strategy in Place

Now that you have a few stocks that are ready to go, you're probably excited to get into the market and start doing you is trading. Before you make that purchase, you need to finish up your strategies. This isn't just the overall strategy but also the center and the exit strategy so you know how to get into and out of the market at the right times.

The first strategy you should work with here is your entry strategy. This is the place where you are comfortable and will purchase your stock. Your aim is to get this entry point as low as you can so that you don't spend too much money and to increase your profits later on. When you look through the charts for that stock, you should be able to figure out a safe entry point that will provide you with a reasonable price on that stock.

You also need to come up with an exit strategy. It is important to have a stop for losing money and one for earning money. First, let's look at the stop for losing money. There are times when the strategies that you pick or the decisions that you make are not going to turn out how you wanted and the stock may start to lose money. The point of this stop is to ensure that you can control how much money you will lose in the process. Once the stock ends up reaching this number, you will withdraw from the market, no matter what the stock does later on.

Without this stop, you could end up with a little bit of trouble. Many new traders see that the stock is going down, and they keep riding it out. They hope that the market will turn around. Sometimes the market will turn around, but then there are times when the market will stay low or keep going down.

Purchase the Stocks You Want

After you created your watch list and came up with your enter and exit strategies to keep you safe, it is time to actually go into the market and make your purchase. You will want to have all the criteria in place for that stock before doing this. But if you are working with a strategy, that is going to outline the criteria for you, so just follow that.

If you plan to work with your broker when doing day trading, you would just give them your order to get the trade started. The order is going to include a ton of information that can help the broker do everything that you want. This would include information on which stocks, in particular, you want to purchase, how many shares of each you want to purchase, how much you will spend on these stocks, when you want to enter the market, and when you want to exit the market. The broker is then able to take that information and place the order for you in the system.

There is also the option for you to do all of the work on your own. This is fine to do, but most beginner traders are not going to pick this option because they worry about messing things up or doing something wrong.

Pay Attention

You will quickly find that day trading has some differences compared to other stock trading options. Many other options are longer-term; you purchase the stock and then ride out the market, hoping that your choice will go up over some time. But with day trading, you are only letting the trade occur in one day. The purchase of the stock, as well as the sale of it, all need to happen sometime between open and close of the same day.

This does make day trading a riskier option to work with compared to some of the other stock trading options. This means that you need to really want the market and make some quick decisions on when to buy and sell your stocks. If you don't watch the market, then how are you going to be able to make these quick changes when needed?

As a day trader, you get to focus on watching these ups and downs that occur during the day. This can make it easier to know when you should purchase a stock in the first place and then it helps you to figure out when you can sell the stocks to make the biggest profits, or to keep your losses to a minimum.

Once you enter into a trade, you need to pay attention to the market and there may be times when the market changes quickly and you will need to make some quick changes to your position, or close it out, to help you earn more profits or keep the losses down as much as possible. Day trading is not one of those methods where you can place the order and then walk away. If you don't have the time to sit and closely watch the market, make sure to not place an order until you have more time.

Sell Your Stocks When They Reach Your Original Exit Points

It is a good idea to listen to your exit point not only when the market is going down but also when the market is going up. Some people understand why they should follow the exit strategy when the market is going down and they do not want to end up losing too much money in the market. It is a bit harder on them when the market is going up. They may have placed a stop for how much profit they wanted to make, but then they see the market still goes up and they do not want to get out at that time.

While it may be hard, make sure that you are listening to your exit strategy, even when the market is going up. Certainly, the market may go past that point, but then it may hit a sharp downturn and you could lose all of that profit. This is another method in place to ensure that your investment stays safe. If the market continues to do well and keeps going up, you will be able to jump back in later on.

Take Some Time to Reflect on That Trade and Write Down Some of the Information as Research Later

As a beginner in the day trading world, there are a lot of things to learn about the market. This is even truer if you have never invested in the past. As a trader, it is your job to learn as you go and make some changes if it is needed. But when you are learning a lot of strategies and keeping track of a large number of trades that are done in day trading, it can be hard to remember everything over time.

Getting a journal and writing down some of your mistakes, your tips, and more after each trade can make a difference.

You don't have to write down a lot of information unless you want to. Just have a few lines or a paragraph. This may seem like it wastes your time. But if you ever get stuck on a trade later on, or if you are trying to figure out why you are in a slump and not getting the profits that you want, looking back through this information can make a big difference in how things go in the future.

Startup Your Second (And Third and Fourth and So on) Trade

Day trading moves very fast. It is likely that your first trade can be done in a few minutes, though as a beginner it will probably take a little bit longer to finish. If there is still time left in the day when you finish up that first trade, then go through these steps again and complete the next trade. Day traders earn a big profit simply by doing a bunch of little trades.

The more of these successful trades that you can get into one day, the more profit you will make. Just make sure that you are following the same steps that we talked about above and take the same precautions that you did with your first trade. If there is not enough time during the day, or you worry that you will rush yourself if you try to do another trade, it is fine to take a break and resume the next day.

There are times when you are going to get into the day trading market and you will make a bad trade in the morning. It may not have gone your way, you may have tried to switch your strategy part way through, or maybe you let your emotions get in the way. If the trade was really bad and you feel upset about it, then it is best to just call it good and take a step away from the market for the rest of the day.

Chapter 4: Thing To Consider Before Your First Trade

How to Control Your Emotions

We associate trading psychology to some behaviors and emotions that are often the triggers for catalysts for decisions. The most common emotions that every trader will come across are fear and greed.

Fear

At any given time, fear represents one of the worst kinds of emotions that you can have. Check-in your newspaper one day, and you read about a steep selloff, and the following thing is trying to rack your brain about what to do following even if it isn't the right action at that time.

Many investors think that they know what will happen in the following few days, which makes them have a lot of confidence in the outcome of the trade. This leads to investors getting into the trade at a level that is too high or too low, which in turn makes them react emotionally.

As the trader puts a lot of hope on the single trade, the level of fear tends to increase, and hesitation and caution kick in.

Fear is part of every trader, but skilled traders have the capacity to manage the fear. There are various types of fears that you will experience, let us look at a few of them:

The Fear to Lose:

Have you ever entered a trade and all you could think about is losing? The fear of losing makes it hard for you to execute the perfect strategy or enter or exit a strategy at the right time.

As a trader, you know that you need to make timely decisions when the strategy signals you to take one. When you be afraid guiding you, the level of confidence drops, and you don't have the ability to execute the strategy the right way, at the right time. When a strategy fails, you lose trust in your abilities as well as strategy.

When you lose trust in many of the strategies, you end up with analysis paralysis, whereby you don't have the capacity to pull the trigger on any decision that you make. Making a move becomes a huge challenge.

When you cannot pull the trigger, all you can think about is staying away from the pain of losing, while you need to move towards gains.

No trader likes to lose, but it is a fact that even the best traders will make losses once in a while. The key is for them to make more profitable trades that allow them to stay in the game.

When you worry too much, you end up being distracted from your execution process, and instead, you focus on the results.

To reduce the fear of trading, you need to accept losses. The probability of losing or making a profit is 50/50, and you need to accept this fact and accept a trade, whether it is a sell or a buy signal.

The Fear of a Positive Trend Going Negative (and Vice Versa):

Many traders choose to go for quick profits and then leave the losses to run down. However, many traders want to convince themselves that they have made some money for the day, so they tend to go for a quick profit so that they have the winning feeling.

So, what should you do instead? You need to stick with the trend. When you notice a trend is starting, it is good to stay with the trend until you have a signal that the trend is about to reverse. It is only then that you exit this position.

To understand this concept, you need to consider the history of the market. History is good at pointing out that times change, and trends can go either way. Remember that no one knows the exact time the trend will start or end; all you need to do is wait upon the signal.

The Fear of Missing Out:

For every trade, you have people that doubt the capacity of the trade to go through. After you place the trade, you will be faced with many skeptics that will doubt the whole procedure, and they will leave you wondering whether to exit the strategy or not.

This fear is also characterized by greed – because you aren't working on the premise of making a successful trade rather the fact that the security is rising without you having a piece of the pie.

This fear is usually based on information that there is a trend that you missed that you would have capitalized on.

This fear has a downside – you will forget about any potential risk associated with the trade and instead think that you have the capacity to make a profit because other people benefited from the action.

Fear of Being Wrong:

Many traders put too much emphasis on being right that they forget that this is a business they should run the right way. They also forget that being successful is all about knowing the trend, and how it affects their engagement.

When you follow the best timing strategy, you create many positive results over a certain time.

The uncanny desire to focus on always being right instead of focusing on making money is a great part of your ego, and to stay on the right path; you need to trade without your ego for once.

If you accommodate a perfectionist mentality when you get into trades, you will be after failure because you will experience a lot of losses as well. Perfectionists don't take losses the right way, and this translates into fear.

Ways to Overcome Fear in Trading:

As you can see, it is obvious that fear can lead to losses. So, how can you avoid this fear and become successful?

- Learn

You need to find a way to get knowledge so that you have the basis for making decisions. When you know all there is to know about options, you know what to buy and when to sell, and learn which ones to watch. You are then more comfortable making the right decisions.

- Have Goals

What are your short term and long-term goals? Setting the right goals helps you to overcome fear. When you have goals, you have rules that dictate how you behave, even in times of fear. You also have a timeline for your journey.

- Envision the Bigger Picture

You always need to evaluate your choices at all times and see what you have gained or lost so far for taking some steps. Understanding the mistakes, you made gives you guidance to make better decisions in the future.

- Start Small

Many traders that subscribe to fear have lost a lot before. They put a lot of funds on the line and ended up losing, which in turn made them fear to place other trades. Begin with small sums so that you don't risk too much to put fear in you. Once you get more confident, you can invest larger sums so that you enjoy more profit.

- Use the Right Strategy

Having the right trading strategy makes it easy to execute your trades successfully. Make sure you look at various options trading strategies so that you know which one is ideal for your situation and skills.

Many strategies can help you succeed, but others might leave you confused. If you have a strategy that doesn't give you the returns you desire, then adjust it to suit your needs over time. Refine it till you are comfortable with its performance.

- Go Simple

When you have a strategy that is simple and straightforward, you will be less likely to lose confidence along the way because you know what to expect.

Additionally, the easier the strategy, the faster it will be to spot any issues.

- Don't Hesitate

At times you have to jump into the fray even if you aren't so comfortable with the way it works. Once you begin taking steps, you will learn more about the trade.

However, you need always to be prepared when taking any trade. The more prepared you are, the easier it will be for you to run successful trades.

• Don't Give Up

Things might not always go as you expect them to do. Remember that mistakes are there to give you lessons that will make you a better trader. When you lose, take time to identify the mistake you made and then correct it, then try again.

Greed

This refers to a selfish desire to get more money than you need from a trade. When the desire to get more than you can usually make takes over your decision-making process, you are looking at failure.

Greed is seen to be more detrimental than fear. Yes, fear can make you lose trades, but the good thing is that you get to preserve your capital. On the other hand, greed places you in a situation where you spend your capital faster than you return it. It pushes you to act when you shouldn't be acting at all.

The Danger of Being Greedy:

When you are greedy, you end up acting irrationally. Irrational trading behavior can be overtrading, overleveraging, holding onto trades for too long, or chasing different markets.

The more greed you have, the more foolish you act. If you reach a point at which greed takes over from common sense, then you are overdoing it.

When you are greedy, you also end up risking way much more than you can handle, and you end up with a loss. You also have unrealistic expectations from the market, which makes it seem as if you are after just money and nothing else.

When you are greedy, you also start trading prematurely without any knowledge of the options trading market.

When you are too greedy, your judgment is clouded, and you won't think about any negative consequences that might result when you make certain decisions.

Many traders that were too greedy ended up giving up after making this mistake in the initial trading phase.

How to Overcome Greed:

Like any other endeavor in trading, you need a lot of effort to overcome greed. It might not be easy because we are talking about human emotions here, but it is possible.

First, you have to know that every call you make won't be the right one at all times. There are times when you won't make the right move, and you will end up losing money. At times you will miss the perfect strategy altogether, and you won't move a step ahead.

Secondly, you have to agree that the market is way bigger than you. When you do this, you will accept and make mistakes in the process.

Hope

Hope is what keeps a trading expectation alive when it has reached reversal. Hope is usually factored in the mind of a trader that has placed a huge amount on a trade. Many traders also go for hope when they wish to recoup past losses. These traders are always hopeful that the following trade will be the best, and they end up placing more than they should on the trade.

This type of emotion is dangerous because the market doesn't care at all about your hopes and will take your money.

Regret

This is the feeling of disappointment or sadness over a trade that has been done, especially when it has resulted in a loss.

Focusing too much on missing trade makes the trader not to move forward. After you learn the lessons after such a loss, you need to understand the mistakes you made then move ahead.

When you decide to let regret to rule your thinking, you start chasing markets with the hopes that you will end up making money on a position by doubling the entrance price.

Chapter 5: Options Day Trading Styles

No matter what style or strategy an options day trader chooses to use, he or she needs to factor in three important components every single time. These elements are:

- **Liquidity.** This factor describes how quickly an option or other asset can be bought and sold without the current market price being affected. Liquid options are more desirable to an options day trader because they trade easier. Illiquid options create more resistance in the ease at which a trader can open or close his or her position. This extends the time needed to complete the transactions involved and thus can lead to a loss for the options day trader.
- **Volatility.** This describes how sensitive the assets attached to the options is to price changes due to external factors. Some assets are more volatile than others. Stocks and cryptocurrencies are volatile assets. Volatility has a great impact on an options day trader's profit margin.
- **Volume.** This describes the number of options being traded at a specific time interval. Volume is an indication of the associated assets price movement on the market because it is a gage of the asset's interest in the market. The higher the volume, the more desirable traders typically are in pursuing an option. Volume is one of the factors that make up open

interest, which is the total number of active options. Active options have not been liquidated, exercised or assigned. If an options trader ignores taking action on options for too long, this can make circumstances unfavorable, which can lead to unnecessary losses. An options trader needs to always be on the ball about closing options positions at the appropriate time.

To take advantage of the options day trading choices listed below, the day trader needs to be very familiar with these factors and how he or she can use them to his or her advantage.

The Resistance Trading Strategy with Options

Breakout describes the process of entering the market when prices move out of their typical price range. For this style of trading to be successful, there needs to be an accompanying increase in volume. There is more than one type of breakout but we will discuss one of the most popular which is called support and resistance breakouts.

The support and resistance method describes the point at which the associated asset price stops decreasing (support) and the point at which the associated asset price stops increasing (resistance). The day trader will enter a long position if the associated asset price breaks above resistance. On the other hand, the options day trader will enter a short position if the associated asset breaks below the supported price. As you can see, the position that the trader takes depends on if the asset is supported or resisted at that new price level. As the asset transcends the normal price barrier, volatility typically increases. This usually results in the price of the associated asset moving in the direction of the breakout.

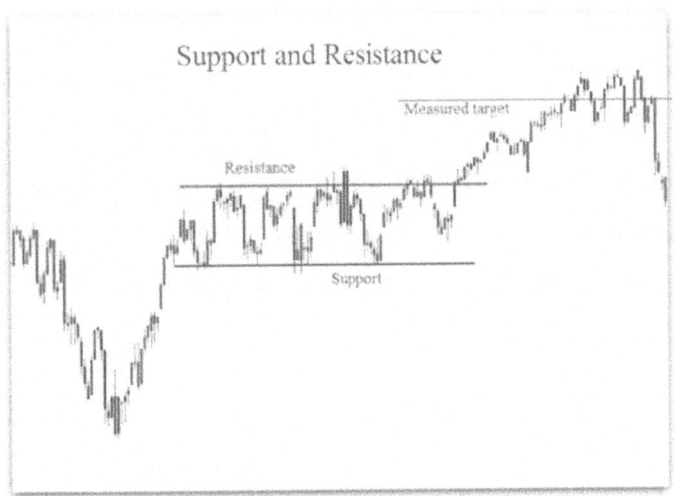

When contemplating this trading style, the options day trader needs to carefully deliberate his or her entry points and exit strategies. The typical entry strategy depends on whether or not the prices are set to close above the resistance level or below the support level. The day trader will take on a bearish position if this price is said to be above the resistance level. A bullish approach is a typical maneuver if prices are set to close below the support.

Exit strategies require a more sophisticated approach. The options day trader needs to consider past performance and use chart patterns to determine a price target to close his or her position. Once the target has been reached, the day trader can exit the trade and enjoy the profit earned.

Momentum Options Day Trading

This options day trading style describes the process of options day trading relying on price volatility and the rate of change of volume. It is so-called because the main idea behind the strategy is that the force behind the price movement of the associated asset is enough to sustain it in the same direction. This is because when an asset increases in price, it typically attracts investors, which drives the price even higher. Options day traders who use this style ride that momentum, and make a profit off the expected price movement.

This style is based on using technical analysis to track the price movement of the associated asset. This analysis gives the day trader an overall picture that includes momentum indicators like:

- The momentum indicator, which makes use of the most recent closing price of the associated asset to determine the strength of the price movement as a trend.
- The relative strength index (RSI), which is a comparison of profits and losses over a set period of time.
- Moving averages, which allows the day trader to see passed fluctuations to analyze the trends in the market.
- The stochastic oscillator, which is a comparison of the most recent closing prices of the associated asset over a specified period of time.

Momentum options day trading is highly effective and simple as long as it is done right. The day trader needs to keep abreast of the news and earnings reports to make informed decisions using this trading style.

What Is Reversal Trading and How this Works

This style relies on trading against the trend and is in essence, the opposite of momentum options day trading. Also called trend trading or pull back trending, it is performed when an options day trader is able to identify pullbacks against the current price movement trends. Clearly, this is a risky move but it can be quite profitable when the trade goes according to plan. Because of the depth of market knowledge and trading experience that is needed to perform this style effectively, it is not one that is recommended for beginners to practice.

This is a bullish approach to options trading and entails buying an out of the money call option as well as selling an out of the money put option. Both profit and loss are potentially unlimited.

Scalping Options Day Trading

This options day trading style refers to the process of buying and selling the same associated asset several times in the same day. This is profitable when there is extreme volatility on the market. The options day trader makes his profit by buying an options position at a lower price then selling it for a higher price or selling an options position at a higher price and buying it at a lower price depending on whether or not this is a call or a put option.

This style of options trading is extremely reliant on liquidity. Illiquid options should not be used with this style because the options day trader needs to be able to open and close these types of trades several times during the space of one day. Trading liquid options allow the day trader to gain maximum profitability when entering and exiting trades.

The typical strategy is to trade small several options during the course of the day to accumulate profit rather than trying to trade big infrequently. Trading big with this particular style can lead to huge losses in the space of only a few hours. This is why this style is only recommended for disciplined options day traders who are content with seeking small, repeated profits even though it is a less risky method compared to the others.

Due to the nature of this style, it is the shortest form of options day trading because it does not even last the whole day – only a few hours. Day traders who practice this style are known as scalpers. Technical analysis is required to assess the best bets with the price movement of the associated assets.

Scalping is an umbrella term that encompasses several different methods of scalping. There is time and sales scalping, whereby the day trader uses passed records of bought, sold and cancelled transactions to determine the best options to trade and when the best times for these transactions are. Other types of scalping involve the use of bars and charts for analysis of the way forward.

Using Pivot Points for Options Day Trading

This options day trading style is particularly useful in the forex market. It describes the act of pivoting or reserving after a support or resistance level has been reached at the market price. It works in much the same way that it does with support and resistance breakouts.

The typical strategies with this particular options day trading style are:

- To buy the position if the support level is being approached then placing a stop just below that level.
- To sell the position if the resistance level is being approached then placing a stop just below that level.

To determine the point of pivot, the day trader will analyze the highs and lows of the previous day's trading and the closing prices of the previous day. This is calculated with this formula:

(High + Low + Close) / 3 = Pivot Point

Using the pivot point, the support and resistance levels can be calculated as well. The formulas for the first support and resistance levels are as follows:

(2 x Pivot Point) – High = First Support Level

(2 x Pivot Point) – Low = First Resistance Level

The second support and resistance levels are calculated with the following formulas:

Pivot Point – (First Resistance Level – First Support Level) = Second Support Level

Pivot Point + (First Resistance Level – First Support Level) = Second Resistance Level

The options trading range that is most profitable lies when the pivot point is between the first support and resistance levels.

The options day trader is vulnerable to sudden price movements with his style of trading. This can result in serious losses if it is not managed. To limit losses with this strategy, the options day trader can implement stops to marginalize losses. This is typically placed just above the recent high price close when the day trader has taken on a short position. This is placed just below a recent low when the day trader had taken on a long position. To be doubly safe, the options day trader can also place two stops, such as placing a physical stop at the most capital that he or she can afford to part with and another where an exit strategy is implemented.

Where these stops are placed is also dependent on volatility.

Chapter 6: Does A Fundamental Analysis Work with Options?

Options trading requires less technical analysis than other trade styles, but you are still required to perform technical analysis to ensure that the market entry point you are looking at is going to be profitable. Entering any market at any time without having first completed proper technical analysis can lead to a greater risk of losses due to not clearly understanding what is likely going to happen with the market in its current state.

When you perform technical analysis your goal is to identify possible positions that you can enter, validate the quality of those positions, choose the position(s) you will take, and then pick the perfect entry point. By following this exact system for entering the market, you can feel confident that you are entering the market at the best possible time, every single time. This way, you maximize your potential for profits and minimize your potential for losses.

Remember, the more educated you are on what you are doing and what position you are taking, the more likely you are going to be able to increase your profits with trading.

Conducting technical analysis for options trading should be completed as a routine every time you do it to ensure that you never miss out on a step. In this manner, you create a strong system that works for validating your positions, and you can always feel confident that you are taking on the best positions possible.

Creating Your Watchlist for Possible Positions

The first thing you need to do when you are engaging in technical analysis is to create a watchlist that is complete with possible trade positions that you can take on that day. You can start identifying possible positions by looking at various stock news sites like the ones I mentioned earlier in this book to help you get a feel for what is going on in the market.

Using these news sites to identify possible positions simply helps by giving you the opportunity to narrow down your scope so that you are only looking at a few places in the market, rather than looking blankly at the market as a whole. This way, you are not spending hours every day scouring for the best possible places.

After you have gauged the market by looking at the news, you can start looking at the market itself to see which positions are looking most favorable. At this point, you can narrow down your listen even further just by getting a simple once over at the market itself. This should help you identify 3-5 positions, or possibly a few more, that may be ideal for you to take on for the day. If you have more than 3-5, start by picking the 3-5 that are most likely to be profitable and conduct your research on these positions, first.

It is likely that you will find your best positions this way, however, if for some reason none of the ones you have looked at seem good you can move on to the next 3-5 options to find a better position.

Validating the Quality of Your Possible Positions

Now that you have located a few possible positions that you could trade-in, you need to start the process of validating which ones are truly going to be a good position for you to hold and which ones are not.

If you are looking at a good position, everything you find out during the research phase should confirm what you already anticipated when you began to look into the position. If the information differs, this does not necessarily mean that it is a bad position, however, it does mean that you are going to have to consider the numbers to decide whether or not it has the capacity to earn you as many profits as you desire.

You also need to decide whether or not you are willing to endure the risk that is being expelled by this particular position in the market.

In addition to validating your spot in the market, conducting this form of research is going to help you start to identify what possible trading strategies you could use with each given position. I recommend using a notebook and writing down your watchlist, and then writing down all of the research and strategy ideas you come up with for each position you are looking into. This way, when you move into picking your actual position you have an easy chart for comparison, and when you move in on an actual trade deal you already have a strategy outlined that you can follow when you get into the market.

With that being said, make sure that you always check which strategy is going to help you leverage each possible position. Knowing what strategy you want to execute when you get into each trade deal will ensure that you are going in with a clearly outlined plan and that you know exactly what you have to do at every point to maximize your profits from that trade.

Choosing Which Position Will Earn Maximum Gains (And Minimize Losses)

Now that you have thoroughly researched how each position is likely to play out and what types of profits you are likely to incur with each one, as well as what risks you are exposed to, you can move into deciding what position you want to take on. Deciding what position you are going to trade in the market is not entirely a science, although there are some things you are going to want to weigh into your consideration to help you make the best decision.

At the end of the day, though, it comes down to how confident you feel in a certain position as your confidence in the position is important. If you feel thoroughly confident that the chances of your chosen position earning you a profit is high, chances are that is the best position for you to take on.

Building your confidence in your trades is an important part of creating a strong trading strategy that you can foster to help you become a better trader.

Aside from your confidence, there are some obvious points you are going to want to consider when it comes to where you position yourself and your trade in the market.

Obviously, you want to make sure that you have chosen a spot that has been validated through your research to prove that you are likely to make profits in that position. You should never gamble on a position in the market, as this can lead to you incurring massive losses during your time in the market which is never a good idea. Also, you should never enter a position if the news surrounding the market is uncertain unless you are intentionally banking on that uncertainty such as with a long straddle position.

However, if you are looking for moderate changes, but a certain stock is tied in with some major news headline, chances are you should avoid that stock as it may not be the best position for you to take on. If you are banking on minimal gains and the stock changes drastically, you could end up in the red because you positioned yourself poorly.

Always make sure that the position you choose is packed with both research and confidence to ensure that you are taking on the best positions possible.

Picking Your Exact Entry Point

The last part of your analysis comes from deciding when your entry point is going to be. At this point, you have already designed your exit strategy during your research phase so now you have to decide on when you are going to enter that position to maximize your gains.

This part cannot be broken down to a science, either, as there is never a way to truly guarantee what the market is going to do or when it is going to do it. Even if you are confident that the market is about to behave in a certain way, you cannot confidently guarantee the exact moment at which that shift is going to happen. For that reason, you truly just need to pay attention to your indicators, follow the pattern, and make your best-educated guess on when the best timing is for you to enter into a new options trader.

As you trade more, you will find that it does become easier for you to understand when and where you should be positioning yourself so that you can enter into better trade deals and earn greater profits. This is one of those skills, however, that comes from building your intuition through regularly engaging with the market and developing an intuitive understanding for how the market works and when the best points of opportunity are.

Even so, you are still bound to make errors by entering the market anywhere from a little bit too soon or late too much too soon or too late. This is normal for every trader, so you will need to recognize this as being a neutral reality of trading and accept it for what it is, to avoid letting it result in you emotionally clinging to your trade deals.

Chapter 7: Tips For Day Trading Option

As an options trader, there are many different types of assets that you can work with, and even different markets that you can enter. Getting started provides you with a lot of choices to help you earn a profit, no matter which direction the market is heading. Use the following tips to make things easier and to help you become more successful with all of your trades.

Always Be Flexible When Trading Options

When you are working with stocks and some of the other securities out there, you will need to do it on the idea of buying low and selling high. But when you are working with options, this approach often doesn't meet all of your needs. With options, you can profit even if the market is going down. Options work well no matter what the market conditions are, either there is a lot of volatility, stagnation, downturns, and upturns. As someone new to the idea of trading, you need to think about all of the different options before you. Always be ready to look at all the various opportunities that are out there, and be prepared to seize them, even in places you may not have considered before. Flexibility is great with this kind of trading because it allows you to see more opportunities and new trading strategies in the process. Options can be a different game compared to what you may be used to with other forms of trading.

If you have been working in the stock market in the past, then you may be unsure about the differences. Make sure that you learn how to trade in options and the differences between stocks and options before you get started with this at all. This ensures that you are ready to take on more opportunities and still earn as many profits as possible.

Use options to hedge and minimize your risk Hedging is a great technique that you can use as an options trader to help to reduce your exposure and reduce some of your risks. So, let's say that you hold onto a stock from a blue-chip company. You are worried about how the stock may end up going down in value in the following weeks. To avoid this disaster, something that could cost you a lot of money, you would instead choose to do a put option. This allows you to sell the shares at market price, even if the cost of your stocks end up dipping. This is an excellent method to use to save your investments and protect your money. The issue of hedging is such a compelling one that many traders will try out options to keep their investments safe. Remember that there isn't any guarantee and it is possible that you could lose out on this for a bit. But the history of options and functional analysis can show that this can help increase your chances of being successful with options.

Working with Break-Even Points

Another thing to consider when it comes to options trading is the break-even points. As a trader, you must understand these break-even points, so you know the best time to get out of a trade, and you don't exit too early and take a loss without even realizing it. The break-even point is often going to be specific, whether it's high or low, that the stock needs to reach before you can start to earn a profit. These break-even points need to also take into account the amount you paid to get into the trade, as well as any fees or costs that you got from your broker to get started. Figuring out your break-even points can help you to avoid some of the shocks later on, and any surprises that come out then. Many times, traders forget to work with the fees and commissions that they have to pay their broker when it comes to the trades. They will only figure out the break-even part based on how much they originally invested. Then, when they take the money out at the break-even point, and they have to pay the commissions and fees, they end up losing money in the process — figuring these numbers out ahead of time and take out all of the surprises. Figure out how much it will cost to get into the trade. Then figure out any extra fees and commissions that you will owe to the brokers when you are all done. From there, you can determine what the break-even point is to get started. You can then move on from here and figure out the point where you can begin to earn a profit and make your plans on whether this is a good trade or not, based on those calculations.

Always Do Your Research

Before you enter into any trade with options, make sure that you do sufficient amounts of research. Charts are going to be crucial when you work on your technical analysis. But this isn't always enough on its own. When you begin, take some time to figure out what kinds of stocks and underlying assets interest you the most, and then do some further research into those particular assets. Take your time to learn about the markets that you want to enter. Watch the charts and find out how they work. Learn the history of those assets, and about the companies that own them. Talk to a broker or someone else who works in the market and get their advice. The more research you can do ahead of time with these options, the easier it will be. You will gain a full understanding of the assets, and be better prepared to make the right decisions when it is time to do your trades. You will find that there are a ton of different sources that you can use to help you do your research and utilizing as many of them as possible can make a big difference in how well you are going to do with your trades in the long run. Before even entering into the market, make sure that you spend at least a few weeks researching the options and their underlying assets that you are most interested in. The more knowledge that you can add to your arsenal, and the better you understand these underlying assets, the better you will be able to do with your trades. With that said, you will need to take some time to find the best resources. You will need to find charts so that you can learn the history of the underlying assets. Find several assets that you would like to work with, and bring out as many historical charts as possible. Then move on to other tables about the industry as a whole, and even the whole market, to see where these underlying assets come from. This helps you to get a good idea of whether it is performing under average, at average, or over average based on how other companies are doing. You shouldn't stop right there, though. You must make sure that you work with additional resources as well. You need to have information from different online sources (make sure that they are reputable and stay up to date), newspapers, and more. You need to know what is going on in the market and the industry, and how that is going to affect any of the different assets that you want to trade-in. You never know when a change in the market can make a significant change in how your options, and their underlying asset, are going to behave.

Going with the Flow

As much as possible, you should go with the flow and do a trend with the trend. With options trading, you will often find that the trend is going to be your friend. This can be true in any investment that you choose to go with, and even seasoned traders know that jumping on the trend, especially early on, is an easy way to make some good money in the market. Any time that you are looking at underlying security and trying to assess its worth, never try to make guesses or estimates. Especially when you are a beginner, these estimates are going to be wrong, and your investing actions are going to be like gambling. But if you trust the trend (which means you have to watch the market and the charts), you will be right most of the time, and you will earn a profit in your trading endeavors.

Your Exit Point, or Your Escape Plan

All successful traders have one thing in common, they have a strategy in place, and they choose to stick with it. They refuse to let their emotions take charge of their trading goals. Feelings are unreasonable and erratic, while a trading plan is thought-out and logical. As part of your trading plan, you must have a clearly defined exit strategy, one that you stick with no matter what. To keep this simple, that exit point is the place where you will close out the trade and walk away if the business starts to head south and you start to lose money. If you follow this, you can protect your investment, and it ensures that you don't stay in the market for too long. But if you let the emotions take control, you can end up losing a lot of money because you remain in the trade too long. Before you ever enter into a business, make sure that you list out your exit points. Know precisely what criteria need to come into play for you to stay in the trade, and which ones you need to follow to leave the business. If you can stick with this, you can limit your losses and ensure that you can make the most profit possible.

Chapter 8: The Psychology Of An Option Trading

Day Trading, like any other form of investment, is subject to influence from human emotion and psychological impact. Whenever money or capital is in play, people tend to take matters rather personally because of the inevitable consequence of the hope that comes along with the promise of significant returns. People will strive to make money while at the same time, avoid circumstances that may cause them to lose their capital. It is from this zero-sum mentality that the influence of psychology or emotions may creep into a sensible mindset. Such control takes over every aspect of the Day Trading instincts that you learned over time.

Your knowledge goes out of the window when a situation that triggers your psychological response arises. A high degree of counterproductivity thus ensues. It, eventually, leads to the dismissal of logical decisions in favor of hunches as well as the need to chase after fleeting profits and cover your previous losses. For you to manage your Day Trading expertise through challenging scenarios, you need to look out for emotions that alter your reasoning capability adversely. Try to improve and nurture a productive mindset, while at the same time, avoid promoting a mental culture that justifies negativity falsely. The following few behaviors and traits are central to your particular mindset whenever you decide to participate in Day Trading:

Do Not Rationalize Your Trading Errors

This mindset t is one of the leading obstacles to the progress and eventual success of your Day Trading endeavors. You are often prone to justify any trading mistakes that you make to the detriment of moving forward. For instance, you get an entry into a particularly promising trade deal later than necessary in spite of your much earlier knowledge of its potential for profitability. The delay causes you to miss an excellent opportunity at the previous entry point. However, you decide to justify this misstep by convincing yourself of your preference for trading late over missing the same deal entirely.

The downside to such delays is often a faulty sense of size estimation in taking your trading position. Hence, the resulting increased exposure to financial risk you become disadvantaged by. Beware of your procrastination when it comes to productive openings that are currently available in Day Trading. If you possess this tendency, consider getting rid of it as soon as possible before it costs you a lot more capital in the long run. In case you are not prone to the frequent postponement of your responsibilities to a later date, be alert for the development of this mentality with the trading company that you keep. You can quickly become influenced by the kind of traders from whom you seek advice on more complex trading strategies. When present, stockbrokers affect your trading ethos, as well.

Poor trading etiquette from these external sources will rub off on you and vice versa. Try to keep the company of well-known responsible trading partners and stockbrokers when the need arises. Another rationalization scenario involves a run of profitable results. Based on a series of trade deals that made you successive returns, you begin to convince your brain of your seemingly high intelligence. This false belief in your skills may lead you to overestimate your trading expertise. Before long, you may start engaging in Day Trading on a hunch rather than apply logic to your decisions. You stop referring to your trusted trading plan and jump into many trading opportunities haphazardly. After a while, these instances of carelessness and trading arrogance will catch up with you because they always inevitably do. Your chances of plunging into a financial disaster go up.

With your eventual financial ruin come the cases of psychological meltdown leading to a negative feedback loop. A wrong decision from your misplaced sense of conceitedness will invariably lead to high-risk exposure. As a result, you suffer significant losses eventually, and consequently, your emotional health suffers, causing you to spiral into a state of depression. This loop is often self-propagating, meaning that it feeds onto itself. Besides, bad decisions lead to adverse outcomes and a fragile mindset, which, in turn, is prone to make more bad decisions, and the loop goes on and on. Keep in mind that in Day Trading, such a feedback loop is often disastrous. All these adverse effects arise from your initial false sense of justification for a wrong deed.

Beware of Your Trading Decisions

This advice is so apparent that it sounds redundant when mentioned. However, decisions are typically the product of your reasoning and judgment at a particular moment. When it comes to decisions on Day Trading, psychological influence is often a determining factor in the process. Keeping your wits about you is very crucial, especially when everything seems to be out of control. You need to realize that every trade has its ups and downs, and how you deal with the challenging times is often more consequential. Try to maintain a logical mindset when making Day Trading choices from a variety of bad options. When it seems that an imminent financial downturn is inevitable, the extent of your loss becomes essential. In this case, you will need to make a sensible decision on the degree of losing margins that you can tolerate adequately.

At this point, you are probably in a state of so many overwhelming emotions that your foggy mental faculties become clouded. An expected human response is to run away from danger, naturally, but in certain situations, fleeing may not be an option. A reflex in a trading scenario often leads to an impulsive decision. Such a choice is, in turn, typically not well thought or deliberative. You should confront your unfavorable circumstances head-on and attempt to fix the situation, however hopeless. This sense of perseverance is usually the essence of most trading excursions, especially when the times become financially rough. Going through the loss of some capital and other Day Trading challenges is often a painful experience that can lead to illogical decisions.

Always remember to uphold vigilance and adhere strictly to the guidelines in your trading plan when confronted with obstacles during your trades. The trading plan usually has instructions on how to handle these seemingly desperate situations. In addition, the prior preparation of any trading guide is generally free of emotional or psychological influence; hence, you can rely on it to maintain neutrality. Also, beware of making trading resolutions when going through a phase with a foul mood. Such conclusions are bound to lead you into a financial catastrophe, especially if you are not careful. Learn to put off the verdict to a time when you can resume logical thinking. When you make any rash decision, it can only result in your further exposure to even more risk.

Keep Your Emotions in Check

Learn to stick to a Day Trading system and method that you trust. Such a strategy may be one that has a history of always making significant returns. Once you master and fully grasp how to apply a specific approach to your trading deals, try to fine-tune it to your preference based on your ultimate objectives. Afterward, stick to this tried, practiced, and tested system in all your searches for valid trade deals. On some days, the stock market may be slow with a low volume of trade. The volatility in such a case is often negligible. However, due to an unchecked emotional influence, you develop a sense of greed or lust for profits.

The desire for benefits on a slow day is common. It leads to the urge to trade on anything to make a small profit. In this situation, you will move from Day Trading into gambling. Trading requires a logical mindset on your part with a lack of psychological attachment whatsoever. Gambling is a consequence of emotional and mental factors running amok in your Day Trading system. If a particular trading style worked on multiple times in the past, teach your brain to consider it. Your trusted trading system will indicate a lack of valid trade opportunities on a specific slow market day. In this case, curb your emotions, desires, and urges to chase a quick profit; however strong they seem.

You should never allow yourself to resort to gambling under any circumstances. Gambling is detrimental to healthy and responsible Day Trading behavior. The risk exposure exponentially rises when you grow accustomed to the desire for profits. If a given day of trading is unfavorable, you should not take part in invalid and unworthy deals. In addition, you should only trade on verifiable opportunities. At certain times, you may experience a series of successive returns in a relatively short period. Learn to know when to stop and how to curb your lust for wanting more returns. Trust your system to trade only on valid deals; however, multiple opportunities are available. An emotion that goes unmonitored in such situations is the greed for more profit.

You convince yourself psychologically that the various deals could be a sign of your lucky day. This mentality in a false belief is wrong, and you need to be aware of it. Your psychology can play deceitful tricks on your logical mind leading to high-risk trading deals. You must realize that in Day Trading, it is almost impossible to get more returns out of a system than what the stock market offers. Emotional corruption also comes into play in a scenario where you bite off more than you can chew.

The greed for substantial amounts of returns may cause you to take high-risk trading positions for a chance at quick profits. However, you must remember that profits and losses are both possible outcomes from a Day Trading session. Therefore, you need to learn to trade in amounts that you can afford to lose. After all, Day Trading involves taking a chance based on a speculative position. You should practice trading in small amounts of money within the confines of low-risk deals. In this case, a potential loss may not be as damaging as the earlier high-risk trading position driven by greed. Eliminate the role of emotions in Day Trading and learn to accept the uncertainty of an unknown future outcome.

Be Patient When Trading

Patience is a crucial trait to have when you take part in Day Trading due to the upswings and downward trends in stock prices. It can become challenging to identify the right entry or exit point for a particular trading opportunity, given the fluctuating nature of a volatile market. However, when you master the art of being patient and studying the trade intently, you can come up with a winning strategy. Having a planned approach is essential, and you should prepare one before engaging in any Day Trading. Often, most seasoned traders include trading strategies for different market conditions in their trading plans. Hence, when making your trading plan, consider incorporating a trading strategy within it.

Chapter 9: Risk Management

Money & Risk Management Techniques

For successful trading in the stock markets, money management and risk management are crucial steps. Stock markets can turn highly volatile at times, and if you are not careful about protecting your money and risk of open trades, you can suffer huge monetary losses.

Therefore, the first step in day trading should be; learn how to reduce trading risk and manage your capital investment so you can tolerate the normal losses in day trading. Money management is like strengthening your defenses so you can survive in the stock market to trade another day. Safe trading practices to protect your money can increase your profits. A lack of it can also double your losses. Money and risk management can be the difference between success and failure of a day trader. Often, beginners are so focused on making profits in stock markets, they forget to protect their invested capital, and soon; their losses wipe out the whole trading capital.

"A penny saved is a penny earned" perfectly explains the money management principle in stock trading. Often, day traders stay in a loss-making trade, thinking soon the losses will stop and the trend will reverse to award them profits. This is the biggest mistake they can do. It is always safer to exit a loss-making trade with a small loss and protect your capital from being wiped out completely. Putting a stop loss in all your trades is the safest way of protecting your trading capital.

Part of good money management is using just a fraction of your trading capital on one trade. In other words, never put all your money on a single trade. As they say, 90% traders do not make profits in day trading. A big reason for this failure is not paying attention to money management. If you keep on betting on stock prices for rising of falling with no proper strategy and risk management, then it is pure gambling and not any intelligent business venture.

Take day trading as a business, do it with proper money management, learn how you can reduce the risk in your trades; you will reduce the number of potential losses, and increase potential profits. Keep your trading cost to a minimum. Before opening any trade, always decide how much loss you will allow for that trade and put a stop loss to cover that much amount. Markets will come back the next day, but you should be left with enough capital to trade when markets open for the next session.

Understanding Margin Trading

Brokerage firms and financial institutions that allow day trading on their platforms, provide margin facility to their clients to trade stocks or other financial assets at a fraction of the original cost. This called margin trading, and it is usually restricted to intraday trade.

With the margin facility, a trader with $20 can trade a share that costs $200. Trading on margin is borrowing funds from the brokerage firm, and trading on that borrowed money for far many times then your money will allow, is not a good idea.

Margin trading allows day traders to trade multiple times in a session with a small investing capital. For prudent day traders, it is a good facility that they use for their profits. But for beginners, it may turn into a trap, making them greedy and losing money by over-trading. Margin facility gives a false sense to day traders of having more money than they have. During trading, they forget that they're trading on borrowed money and sometimes, accumulate more losses. Also, the brokerage charges pile up and total losses for them become higher than the money in the account. In such situations, traders get a call from their brokerage, demanding to deposit money in their accounts to cover the deficit. This is known as the "margin call', and is a signal that the trader is accumulated losses.

Like nuclear power, margin trading can be good in experienced hands and destructive in the hands of novice traders who become greedy for its power.

Therefore, margin trading should be done in a calculated way. Traders should keep an account of how many trades they have done in a single session and how much loss or profits they have made.

Margin facility is good for those traders who have strict rules for money management and control over their trading habits. By trading carefully, they can increase their profits with just a small investment. Trading on margin increases a trader's trading power because with the help of margin they can trade for a greater amount than the money in their trading accounts will allow. If your brokerage firm offers merging facility for day trading, consider and plan carefully how you will use it before taking any decision.

In margin trading, all open positions are squared off before markets close for that session and traders are not allowed to carry forward positions that have been opened using the margin facility.

Manage Market Risk

When people think of day trading, they only think of potential profits, not losses. Therefore, day trading attracts so many people that don't see the risk of losses. In stock markets, various events can trigger losses for investors and traders, which are beyond their control. These events can be economic conditions such as recession, geopolitical changes, also, changes in the central bank policies, natural disasters, or sometimes terror attacks.

This is the market risk; the potential of losing money due to unknown and sudden factors. These factors affect the overall performance of stock markets, and regardless of how careful one is while day trading, the possibility of market risk is always present, which can cause losses. The market risk is known as the systematic risk because it influences the entire stock market. There is also a nonsystematic risk, which affects only a specific industry or company. Long-term investors tackle this risk by diversification in their investment portfolio.

Unlike investors, day traders have no method to neutralize market risk, but they can avoid it by keeping track of financial and business events, news, and economic calendars. For example, stock markets are very sensitive to the central banks' rate policies and become highly volatile on those days. Nobody knows what kind of policy any central bank will adopt in its monetary meeting. But day traders can check the economic calendar and know which day these meetings will take place. They can avoid trading on those days and reduce the risk of loss in trading.

Therefore, knowledge of stock markets and being aware of what is happening in the financial world is essential for day traders. Many successful traders have a policy of staying away from trading on days when any major economic event will take place, or a major decision will be announced. For example, on the day when the result of an important election is declared; any big company's court case decision comes in, or a central banks' policy meeting takes place. On such days, speculative trading dominates stock markets and market risk is very high. Similarly, on a day when any company announces earnings results, its stock price fluctuates wildly, increasing the market risk in trading of that stock.

For inexperienced day traders, the best way to tackle market risk is to avoid trading on such days.

Risk Management Techniques

In day trading, there is always a risk that you will lose money. Now, if you want to start day trading as a career, learn a few techniques that will reduce and manage the risk of potential losses. By taking steps to manage the risk, you reduce the potential day trading losses.

To stay in the day trading business for the long term, you must protect your trading capital. By reducing the risk of losses, you open the possibilities of future profits and a sustainable day trading business.

If you plan well, prepare your trading strategies before starting to trade; you increase the possibility of a stable trading practice which can lead to profits. Therefore, it is essential to prepare your trading plans every day, create trading strategies and follow your trading rules. These three things can make or break your day trading business. Professional day traders always plan their trades first and then trade their plans. This can be understood by an example of two imaginary traders. Suppose there are two traders, trading in the same stock market, trading the same stock. One of them has prepared his trading plan and knows when and how he will trade. The other trader has done no planning and is just sitting there, taking the on-the-spot decisions for buying or selling the stock. Who do you think will be more successful? The one who is well prepared, or the one who has no inkling of what he will do the next second?

The second risk management technique is using stop orders. Use these orders to decide to fix your stop -loss and profit booking points, which will take emotions out of your decision-making process, and automatically cut the losses or book the profit for you.

Many a time, profitable trade turns into loss-making because markets change their trend, but traders do not exit their positions, hoping to increase profits. Therefore, it is necessary to keep a profit booking point and exit the profitable trades at that point. Keeping a fix profit booking point can also help you calculate your returns with every trade and help you avoid taking the unnecessary risk for further trades.

Taking emotions out of day trading is a very important requirement for profitable trading. Do not prejudge the trend in stock markets, which many day traders do and trade against markets, ending with losses.

Using Risk-Reward Ratio

Day trading is done for financial rewards and the good thing is, you can always calculate how much risk you take on every trade and how much reward you can expect. The risk-reward ratio represents the expected reward and expected risk traders can earn on the investment of every dollar.

The risk-reward ratio can excellently indicate your potential profits and potential loss, which can help you in managing your investment capital. For example, a trade with the risk-reward ratio of 1:4 shows that at the risk of $1, the trade has the potential of returning $4. Professional traders advise not to take any trade which has a risk-reward ratio lower than 1:3. This indicates, the trader can expect the investment to be $1, and the potential profit $3.

Expert traders use this method for planning which trade will be more profitable and take only those trades. Technical charting is a good technique to decide the risk-reward ratio of any trade by plotting the price moment from support to resistance levels. For example, if a stock has a support level at $20, it will probably rise from that level because many traders are likely to buy it at support levels. After finding out a potential support level, traders try to spot the nearby resistance level where the rising price is expected to pause. Suppose a technical level is appearing at $60. So, the trader can buy at $20 and exit when the price reaches $60. If everything goes right, he can risk $20 to reap a reward of $60. In this trade, the risk-reward ratio will be 1:3.

By calculating the risk-reward ratio, traders can plan how much money they will need to invest, and how much reward they can expect to gain from any trade. This makes them cautious about money management and risk management.

Some traders have a flexible risk-reward ratio for trading, while others prefer to take trades only with a fixed risk-reward ratio. Keeping stop-loss in all trades also helps in managing the risk-reward ratio. Traders can calculate their trade entry point to stop-loss as the risk, and trade entry to profit as the reward. This way, they can find out if any trade has a bigger risk than the potential reward or a bigger reward than the potential risk. Choosing trades with bigger profits and smaller risks can increase the amount of profit over a period.

Chapter 10: Trading Tools And Platforms

An imperative part of alternatives exchanging is the stage that one uses to exchange. This is on the grounds that choices exchanging requires observing and requires a constant examination of patterns. Execution is likewise observed, and since the exchange is affected upon by a complex of components, one needs to pick a reasonable stage for exchanging.

A decent stage for exchanging should offer a great deal of chances for brokers. These are chances to situate fledglings into exchanging, improvement for the current ones, and completion for those with a record on the stage. A foundation of exchanging should likewise recommend the accessible items and any assets that supporters on the stage can profit by to drive themselves to gainfulness.

With the innovation creating at fast, stages keep on improving continuously. This is both convoluting the exchanging itself just as giving roads of spreading mindfulness about the business. A stage should, in this way, can offer the most ideal experience for the dealers to do a exchange, and become both in experience and returns without meeting plenty of stage restrictions and dissatisfactions.

A Platform Takes Trading to the Holders

Exchanging includes a lot of complexities that may now and again be alarming. It causes individuals to lose enthusiasm when they create it. They see it as excessively confused. The impression is that it is an endeavor implied for the individuals who have a higher perception of ideas in the financial aspects forte and that the individuals who don't a foundation around there will experience issues jumping aboard.

In any case, an exchanging stage needs to introduce choices exchanging as an endeavor that is conceivable and in which anybody with intrigue can prevail. The days when choices exchanging and some other types of exchanging were introduced as a demonstration of advancement are a distant memory. In this time, each area of venture is being depicted as could reasonably be expected, and organizations are presently being made simpler to make a superior possibility for individuals to set out. A stage that limits venture so a lot and is selective as far as how it does its exchanging exercises is unimportant to current financial examples.

Stages, along these lines, must be intuitive and easy to understand. They ought to be able to urge clients to feel like they can deal with the exchange. It ought to likewise have the ability to measure the degree of utilization and give input about how well they can utilize it. On the off chance that it is a site, for example, it must have the option to report the numbers as individuals visit it and what number of in the end wind up making records and exchanging. Tallying traffic is fundamental for criticism that can prompt the production of a superior encounter for the clients.

Rivalry

The purpose behind considering a decent stage is on the grounds that the opposition is high today. The rivalry has prompted the production of better exchanging encounters through development. Stages are currently attempting to out-do each other in being the roads of alternatives exchanging. They are doing this by endeavoring to make methods of improving client experience. It is in this manner fundamental to recognize the different parameters of looking at the stages. In the long run, one needs to pick a stage that offers ideal access to the exchanging scene.

In picking a stage now and again, one would need to exploit the benefits of various stages. This is seeing one's style of exchanging and how they wish to screen their business and check whether a stage is increasingly straightforward in taking care of the tares or whether it offers an away from of controlling buys and sells of alternatives. This is the motivation behind why the different stages must be surveyed as far as their latent capacity. Ordinarily, stages are identified with the instruments of exchanging. A portion of the instruments of exchanging can be discovered right on the foundation of exchanging.

At the point when a foundation of exchanging additionally has different apparatuses of helping exchanging, it guarantees that one can increase a great deal of advantages at one spot. This makes the stage a utility stage where an individual can visit for additional reasons than simply exchanging. It likewise improves it. For example, if a stage has recordings that offer exchanging instructional exercises. This can make it ingenious in giving competency in taking an interest in the very area that the stage works.

To best profit by rivalry, one needs to comprehend the kind of exchange they need to do. This is by naming their cost and measuring which stage can serve better in guaranteeing returns and worth age. This is so as to abstain from going into exchanging distress, and one must show restraint to check whether the stage can likewise come out and meet a dealer at their place of capacity and furthermore help in exchanging solace where the hazard is at the very least.

Watchlist and Scanners

I converse with new brokers pretty much each and every day. I converse with several brokers each month. One of the normal difficulties that new dealers notice doesn't have the foggiest idea what to exchange. A huge number of stocks are moving in the market each and every day, except finding an arrangement that is both reliable and a solid match is extremely hard.

Chapter 11: Build You Trading Strategies

Building Your Own Routine

When you start out trading, I strongly advise you to start out by building your own routine right from day one. Take the time to decide what time you like to check in on the markets, when you are going to start your watchlist and technical analysis, and how you are generally going to engage in trading.

If you need to set alarms each morning to alert you throughout the day, make that a part of your routine. If you like to sit down with a cup of coffee and your tablet so you can check in on the market each morning, make that a part of your routine. If you like to check in on your lunch break and your afternoon break, make that a part of your routine.

Creating a routine in trading is less about having a frivolous schedule to follow and more about instilling strong habits into your trade strategy from the very beginning so that you always make the best moves possible. This way, you can feel confident that you will not miss out on the best positions, mismanage your trades, or forget about your trades and have them canceled at the end of the trading day.

As a result, you will be able to feel more confident in your trading and trade management strategies while also continually improving your strategies as you go.

The 30% Rule

Lastly, I present to you the 30% rule. The 30% rule has less to do with your bottom line and actual trade strategy and more to do with your money management strategy. When it comes to trading as a way to earn any form of income, even a passive income, you want to make sure that you are never cashing out on more profits than you can reasonably handle.

The idea with trading is that you will create profits that increase the amount of investment capital over time, meaning that you can afford to make larger investments and therefore earn larger profits from your trades. With that being said, you do want to make sure that you are cashing out on some of your capital to ensure that you are always earning an income from this strategy which makes it worthwhile. The 30% rule states that you never take more than 30% of the profits that you earn from each trade out of your trading account. So, if you invest $50 into a trade and earn $150 from it, your profit is $100.

First of all, we would point out that the whole guide was written without relying on any kind of fees. As we already mentioned, fees vary, and every brokerage house has its own rules about it.

- Trading options have significant risks. If you are absolutely inexperienced with trading, we would recommend talking with a financial advisor before making any decision.
- Always keep in mind that every investment has its own risk and reward rating which means that if the risk is high, the reward will be high too.

- Expiration date of American style options and European style options (the most commonly used ones) is always the third Saturday in the month for American and the last Friday before the third Saturday for European options.
- Phrase "in the money" describes that the option has a value higher than the strike price for call options and lower than the strike price for put options at the time of their expiration.
- The most common minimal bid for option sharing is one nickel or 5 dollars per contract. However, some more liquid contracts allow minimal bid to be one dollar per contract.
- 100 shares of the certain stock are actually 1 option contract
- If you pay 1 dollar for an option your premium for that option whether you buy or sell it is 1 dollar per share, which means that the option premium is 100 dollars per contract
- All of the examples in this guide assume that every option order ever mentioned was filled successfully.
- Whenever you want to open a new position you will have to sell or buy on the market to "open". The same principle applies if you wish to close your position. You sell or buy to "close".
- Phrase Open Interest represents the number of option contracts that are opened at the moment. Logically- more opened contracts mean a bigger number and closed contracts mean a smaller number.
- Volume of the options is the number of contracts that are traded in one single day.

Be careful when signing the contracts; make sure you read all of the trading options.

So here we are at the end of this guidebook on trading options. They can be extremely profitable but learning to trade them well takes time. You can choose to use indicators to determine your entry points, and I'm all for this approach at first but remember that over the long term, you're better served learning the basics of order flow and using that.

There is no shortage of options strategies you can use to dramatically limit your risk and depending on the volatility levels, you can deploy separate strategies to achieve the same ends. Contrast this with a directional trading strategy where you have just one method of entry, which is to either go short or go long, and only one way of managing risk, which is to use a stop loss.

Spread or market neutral trading puts you in the position of not having to care about what the market does. In addition, it brings another dimension of the market into focus, which is volatility. Volatility is the greatest thing for your gains and options allow you to take full advantage of this, no matter what the volatility situation currently is.

Options can be a bit hard to get your head around at first since so many of us are used to looking at the market as a thing that goes up or down. Options bring a sideways and a different vertical element to it via spreads and volatility estimates. More advanced options strategies take full advantage of volatility and are more math-focused, so if this interests you, you should go for them.

That being said, do not assume the complexity means more gains. The strategies shown here are quite simple and they will make you money thanks to the way options are structured. They bring you the advantage of leverage without having to borrow a single cent.

You can choose to borrow, of course, but you need to do this only if it is in line with your risk management math. Risk management is what will make or break your results and at the center of quantitative risk management is your risk per trade. Keep this consistent and line up your success rate and reward to risk ratios, and you'll make money as a mathematical certainty.

Qualitative risk management requires you to adopt the right mindset with regards to trading, and it is crucial for you to adopt this as quickly as possible. Remember that the implications of your risk math mean that you need not be concerned with the outcome of a single trade. Instead, seek to maximize your gains over the long term.

The learning curve might get steep at times, but given the rewards on offer, this is a small price to pay. Keep hammering away at your skills, and soon you'll find yourself trading options profitably, and everything will be worth it. How much can you expect to make trading options?

I'm not keen on putting numbers to this sort of thing. Generally, a good options trade can expect around 50-80% returns on their capital. As you grow in size, this return amount will decrease naturally. However, to start off with these are beyond excellent returns.

Always make sure you're well capitalized since this is the downfall of many traders. You need to be patient with the process. A lot of people rush headfirst into the market without adequate capitalization or learning and soon find that the markets are far tougher than they thought. So always ensure the mental stress you place yourself in is low and that you're never in a position where you 'have' to make money trading.

Conclusion

Hone your intuition: If you hope to be a successful day trader then you are going to need to get into the habit of making popular trades before they become popular for the best results. As such, you need to get into the habit of always following the beat of your own drum when it comes to drawing conclusions from your research and acting accordingly. While this doesn't mean listening to your gut, if you have put in the time and done the work and it all points in a direction that no one else has gone in yet then you need to be confident enough in your abilities to get in before things turn in that direction and you miss out on profits that were by all rights yours to lose. Knowing when to separate yourself from the pack is what separates average day traders from rich ones.

While this sounds relatively straightforward in theory, in practice, it is much more often about understanding when a certain trade is being hyped by those with something to gain and when the facts are actually pointing in a specific direction. While the most surefire way to learn the difference is through experience, eventually you will be able to determine the difference between a good trade and a good story and make money off the sheep who aren't aware there is a difference in the process. If you are having trouble believing in yourself in this way, then the best way to bolster your confidence is to

Start with listening to your intuition on smaller trades.

The success of any type will make it easier to trust yourself on more important trades in the future and should be celebrated appropriately to ensure they will be remembered the next time a similar situation arises. Remember, just because you are trading in short time frames doesn't mean you need to rush the decisions you make, only by fully thinking through every decision that you make will you know that you have truly made the right decision. A rash decision is a surefire way to lose money, no two ways around it.

Never let your losses build As a new trader, it can be easy to become emotionally invested in the stocks you choose which is why it is crucial that you learn to separate your expectations for a trade from the reality of what occurs when the rubber meets the road. To successfully ensure that you don't lose more than the bare minimum on a given trade it is important that you cut it to lose the second it stops generating a profit as opposed to hanging on to it in hopes that it turns around and rebounds in the correct direction.

It is important to learn early that a failed trade is not a reflection on you as a trader but simply a part of the natural trading process. Sticking with a losing trade is rarely, if ever, going to result in that trade turning around, and if it does the results are going to be middling at best. Likewise, it is never a good idea to double down on a losing trade as a means of mitigating a potential loss. Adding to a losing position is akin to trying to dig yourself out of a hole, it is never going to work no matter how hard you want it to.

Understand that sometimes the market simply has nothing to offer: when many new traders get into the habit of buying up stocks, they feel as though they need to keep it up, even if the market isn't presenting anything worthwhile at the moment. It is important to understand that quality is going to supersede quantity every single time. Making changes to the stocks you are holding too often can easily decrease your profit margins, and hurt your trading plan in the process as it will be difficult to determine just how effective you are actually being. Rather, it is always a better choice to simply let your current investments matriculate and wait until something actually better comes along before you do anything rash.

Don't give in to fear: Besides anger, the most commonly felt emotion while trading is fear. Fear is particularly devious as it can skew your perspective in such a way that it is difficult to do anything but watch as a previously solid trade crumble for no discernible reason. Like anger, it is natural to be a little fearful when it comes to making big trades, especially those of the high risk, high reward variety. Additionally, if you are heavily invested in a specific currency to the point where you perhaps used funds that had other uses, then watching the progress of a given trade once it has been made, is always sure to be a little nerve-wracking.

While being angry can easily cloud your judgment, being afraid can leave you feeling paralyzed, unable to make the types of split-second decisions that can reverse a major loss and turn it to little more than a simple bump in the road. There are two big ways to get over your fears, the first of which is by carefully considering the trades you do make so that you can remain confident throughout and the second is to practice, practice, practice as the more you do so the more comfortable the entire process will feel.

While sticking to your plan, even when your emotions are telling you to ignore it, is the mark of a successful trader, this in no way means that you must blindly follow your plan 100 percent of the time. You will, without a doubt, find yourself in a situation from time to time where your plan is going to be rendered completely useless by something outside of your control. You need to be aware enough of your plan's weaknesses, as well as changing market conditions, to know when following your predetermined course of action is going to lead to failure instead of success. Knowing when the situation really is changing, versus when your emotions are trying to hold sway is something that will come with practice, but even being aware of the disparity is a huge step in the right direction.

Avoid trades that are out of the money: While there are a few strategies out there that make it a point of picking up options that are currently out of the money, you can rest assured that they are most certainly the exception, not the rule. Remember, the options market is not like the traditional stock market which means that even if you are trading options based on underlying stocks buying low and selling high is just not a viable strategy. If a call has dropped out of the money, there is generally less than a 10 percent chance that it will return to acceptable levels before it expires, which means, that if you purchase these types of options what you are doing is a little bit better than gambling, and you can find ways to gamble with odds in your favor of much higher than 10 percent.

Understand the difference between implied volatility and historical volatility: When looking to trade successfully, implied volatility should generally be one of the primary ways to determine if a given asset is priced correctly. Generally, the greater the amount of implied volatility, the more bearish the market will become and the more expensive most assets will be. However, historical volatility is just as important when it comes to choosing profitable trades.

Historical volatility should also be determined beforehand so you can decide if the difference warrants further study. If this turns out to be the case then you are going to want to take the time to go back at least 12 months with the underlying asset in the question in order to get a good baseline for the current state of things. While this can be time-consuming, it will ultimately be worthwhile if you find out things are not as they initially seemed.

Focus on yourself: If you are looking for a way to lose money while day trading, there will never be a more effective means of doing so than by trying to follow the trading plans that work for other people. A trading plan is an extremely personal expression of your goals for the market of your choice and the way that you are going to interact with it. As such, it requires plenty of trial and error, as well as personal introspection to ensure that it works with your natural trading tendencies as opposed to against them.

While looking at the level of success that professional traders have can make it difficult to forge your path, mimicking what they are trying to do is only going to ultimately prove to be an exercise in futility. It is important to instead avoid the temptation by keeping in mind that knowing yourself and your strengths and weaknesses is the most reliable path to success.

Always consider the source of tips: As a new day trader, you will likely be on the lookout for potential trading advice from anywhere and everywhere you can find it. This is a perfectly natural response to the magnitude of possible opportunities out there, and it can even be fruitful in the long run, but only if you know whose tips you should trust and whose you should take with a grain of salt. Many dubious tips start off from an honest place, someone you know who is talking about a company that is soon going to do something like releasing a new killer product, have groundbreaking earnings, or who is going to be purchased by a major conglomerate.

Additionally, you will find many financial personalities on television touting this type of asset or another as the be-all and end-all of trading. While occasionally these types of tips will pay out, in general, the financial personality will have a stake in the investment or it will turn out to just be the new fad for the next few months before it is forgotten entirely. This is not to say that you should avoid all trading tips entirely, rather it is to point out that before you go ahead and make a move you are going to want to do your own research on the investment and then move forward only if you feel the reasoning behind the investment is sound.

Don't underestimate performance reports: A performance report for a trading plan or strategy is an overall measurement of that plan or system's performance. By generating a performance report, you can look at your rules regarding trades to determine how it would have done in a historical context. Also known as backtesting, this is a valuable trading tool for those who want to see how a new system might work before putting it into action or to determine if a new system's performance is a fluke or if it is worth looking into further or discarding all together. A majority of the most common analysis platforms on the market generate performance reports based on backtesting or as you trade in real-time.

www.ingramcontent.com/pod-product-compliance
Lightning Source LLC
Chambersburg PA
CBHW050244220526
45465CB00002B/543